Priority

Your

Time

Daniel Ollivier

KOGAN PAGE

Kogan Page is the UK member of the Euro Business Publishing Network.
The European members are:
Les Editions d'Organisation, France; Verlag Moderne Industrie, Germany;
Liber, Sweden; Franco Angeli, Italy; and Deusto, Spain.
The Network has been established in response to the growing demand for
international business information and to make the work of Network authors
available in other European languages.

Les Editions d'Organisation, 1993
Translated by Ann Leonard
Illustrated by Sool Sbiera

First published in France in 1993 by
Les Editions d'Organisation, 1 rue Thénard, 75240 Paris, Cédex 05,
entitled Vous et .... Vos Priorités, Gérez Votre Temps, ISBN 2-7081-1554-5

This edition first published in Great Britain in 1994 by
Kogan Page Ltd, 120 Pentonville Road, London N1 9JN.

British Library Cataloguing in Publication Data.
A CIP record for this book is available from the British Library.

ISBN 0 7494 1195 3

DTP for Kogan Page by
Jeff Carter 197 South Croxted Road, London SE21 8AY

Printed in Great Britain by
Biddles Ltd, Guildford and Kings Lynn

TABLE OF CONTENTS

The following symbols are used throughout this book to indicate:

 Find your way.

 Fill it in.

INTRODUCTION

> *'The trilogy of knowledge, ability and the will to succeed...'*

A common feature for those of us who enjoy a certain amount of organizational autonomy at work is the difficulty of managing priorities. With crowded schedules and overload signs flashing over our heads how do we cope with the demands for quality and productivity and still keep up the development of our own skills? How do we stem this tide of information while feeding the exchange requirements of our professional environment? How do we prepare for forthcoming events without compromising our treatment of urgent matters?

With all assignments assuming importance, a smoothly running work schedule seems impossible.

Supply can no longer meet demand; there just aren't enough hours in the day. As the number of demands on our time increases so the means to deal with them tends to decline.

Is there a solution to this situation? The temptation to reply in the negative seems great. However, counter to popular consensus, there is often someone at work who seems able to meet all demands, the exception to the rule. It may be that colleague who, under the same working conditions, somehow manages to organize his schedule and still give the impression of being available.

This being the case, we have to concede that some of us achieve more than others. Organizing priorities becomes a highly desirable exercise. So with this in mind we have devised this practical guide to examine how we can prioritize effectively and achieve more.

YOUR CURRENT PROCEDURE

What characterizes your present system of organization? Answer the following statements spontaneously:

STATEMENTS	YES	NO
1. In your daily routine urgency is synonymous with priority.		
2. The time factor frequently decides your choice of method.		
3. At the beginning of the day you have no trouble working out your priority assignments.		
4. Your partners (superiors, colleagues...) know your current projects and priorities.		
5. In your profession, priorities are constantly changing as no two days are ever the same.		
6. The demands made by your boss are such that there is often an increased number of tasks to be done.		
7. The length of time you schedule for any given matter is frequently accurate.		
8. At work, objectives aimed at the medium and short term serve as a permanent reference.		
9. Priorities are time-linked rather than linked in order of actual importance.		
10. No efficient system can be introduced without a complete follow-up programme.		
TOTAL		

DID SOMEONE SAY PRIORITY?

The absence of time out for reflection creates a crisis management situation, rather than a systemized procedure which aims at objectives in the medium and short term.

The main obstacle in the path of success is force of habit. Take dealing with correspondence as an example: we automatically deal with the urgent before the important, the brief before the time-consuming, the pleasant...

In this way important and/or complicated matters get deferred to a later date, before becoming urgent and therefore, finally, priority.

This is a surprising paradox when we know that logic dictates that our system of priorities be organized around URGENCY and IMPORTANCE. Sometimes these notions get confused to the point where we are no longer capable of distinguishing between the necessity to act quickly (imminent deadline) and what is at stake in a given situation. In the face of such confusion the word priority becomes synonymous with urgent.

This reality explains why a system of organizing priorities is tolerated rather than welcomed, why it focuses on the short term rather than the medium term, urgent matters more than important ones.

Answering the phone always takes precedence over the critical analysis of our system of organization. Satisfying a director's or external visitor's demands frequently causes us to shelve scheduled assignments.

It seems then that there is overkill in the use of urgency as a criterion, and this distracts us from our line of action. In a bid to make life easier, a well-known multinational organization coded its usage, *** for immediate attention, ** by lunchtime, *today. This strategy did not have the desired effect. In the absence of a rational approach to urgency, the management of priorities became impossible.

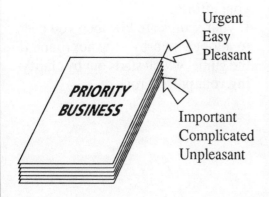

Urgent
Easy
Pleasant

Important
Complicated
Unpleasant

PRIORITY BUSINESS

That being the case we still have to admit to the supremacy of URGENCY over IMPORTANCE. Processing correspondence illustrates this perfectly. The most common method consists of separating the day's tasks from those which can be dealt with at a later date.

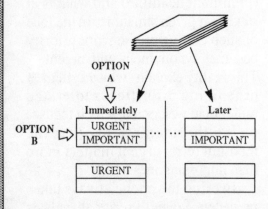

In *option A*, 'important' tasks are always deferred in favour of 'urgent' tasks. This increases the volume of tasks which are both urgent and important. This reality is easily explained: it is easier for us to recognize what is urgent rather than what is IMPORTANT. For want of analysis, importance is often an abstract notion, devoid of meaning. Since everything seems important nothing can really be so. This situation bolsters the position of the urgent at the top of our list of priorities...

In *option B* organizing priorities is based on the criterion of importance. This procedure accommodates the demands of both the medium and short terms. It shows exactly the procedure you need to adopt with the aid of the structures and techniques outlined in this guide.

• •

INTERPRETING THE RESULTS

• •

If your replies are negative for statements 1, 5, 6 and positive for the others, you have mastered the principle of MANAGING PRIORITIES. You may want to devise your own approach to tackling the various sections of this book to gain maximum return for your efforts.

If your scores are low then you need to adopt a step-by-step approach to the guide, which starts out by clarifying your present role.

Section 1
CLARIFYING YOUR PRESENT ASSIGNMENT

> *'The duties define the job...'*

An efficient system of prioritizing should not be at the mercy of events as they crop up. On an individual as well as a collective scale the capacity for managing situations depends on the existence of an operational strategy. To illustrate this, take a look at the case of Mr Woods. He belongs to that category of person who, after many years in the same job, has acquired the necessary expertise to render him effective. For seven years he has been employed as an assistant in an administrative service department of ten people. His job description hasn't been modified since his appointment.

For all that, however, his professional situation is not so cosy. Mr Woods cannot remember a time when he felt so strongly the inadequacy of the means at his disposal. It is true to say that the economic outlook is bleak. The number of staff in his department has been cut by 20 per cent in the last two years while the demands for top quality remain constant.

Peter Woods is first to arrive in the morning and often the last to leave. In this way, he says he can work in peace. However, this situation doesn't solve his organizational problems. His contention is simple: no matter what he does, his workload far outweighs the means available to him for dealing with it. So how can he avoid falling into the time-shortage syndrome?

Called upon by the rest of the personnel from the time he arrives, he is consistently bombarded with phone calls and visits from his superiors.

This seems perfectly normal to him as he is responsible for the supervision and coordination of operations. Some of his associates would like a greater degree of autonomy but Peter doesn't think they're up to it yet.

The team often reproaches him for his lack of availability. But how can he be otherwise? He has to look into an urgent customer demand, attend impromptu meetings or give technical assistance to a colleague. Lack of time is to blame if the files pile up on his desk. Not having the time to read or sort his documentation, he is often obliged to devote great energy searching for a missing item of information. Meanwhile certain documents given to him for signing are left for several days.

So many things seem important that priorities are difficult to define. Peter is not happy with the situation. He regrets, for instance, being unable to respect appointment times with suppliers. This is detrimental to the company's corporate image, as some suppliers have to wait up to an hour before being seen. This hardly makes life easy for his secretary.

Despite progress, internal organization within companies has hardly changed in recent years. Yet every day, the same instructions are repeated and the same duties performed. It's an endless cycle. Peter fails to understand the careless attitude of some individuals. Meetings raise little interest. The long working hours no doubt explain the absenteeism and latent aggression within the group.

At a moment's notice Peter often has to fill in for his boss Robert Murray in handling claims. They are increasing. He has to act quickly as the management frowns on the slightest delay.

The team's training has been neglected for the last few months but how can you really be expected to take part in seminars with such a backlog of work building up? To make matters worse, the team has now refused to work any more overtime. Woods feels particularly isolated because his boss has just been appointed to a new post.

Peter Woods readily admits to feeling powerless and drained at the end of the working day. He can't even bring himself to indulge in his favourite game – tennis.

PERSONAL CONCLUSIONS

What would you choose as your three main recommendations if you were in a position to give advice to Peter Woods?

1. Look for an interview with your superiors to renegotiate the responsibilities of your position...
2. Refuse to carry out certain tasks in order to create awareness among the other team members and the management...
3. Immediately cut down your attendance hours as no one should think themselves indispensable...
4. Rearrange your timetable as there must be 'slow' periods when the assistant's presence isn't required...
5. Close your door to visitors in order to concentrate on priority business...
6. Have phone calls monitored in order to ensure a better allocation of the workload...
7. Employ the secretary's skills more effectively in a system of organizing priorities...
8. Ask your bosses to define your role so as to clarify what is a priority and what isn't...
9. Slot in some relaxation moments during the day in order to cope better with fatigue and stress...
10. Establish a coordination plan with your team in order to cut down on time wasting...
11. Explain the procedure of the various system operations as they represent, by definition, unproductive time...
12. Limit your participation in external meetings...
13. Learn to carry forward customer demands in order to ensure a smoother running work schedule...
14. Sort and file documentation...
15. Check on the allocation of tasks and roles...
16. Conduct an objective analysis of your role in order to determine your priorities…
17. Pay attention to the communication of instructions in order to avoid errors and omissions...
18. Have regular team meetings to share the concerns of organization...
19. Negotiate more realistic targets with the management...
20. Invest in your own technical training. After all, the effects of outdated skills touches every one of us...
21. Establish a training plan in order to delegate duties more effectively...
22. Summarize the current situation and outline any possible improvements...
23. Look for more extensive delegation of responsibilities...
24. Define clear and precise objectives for the coming months...
25. Take a holiday to revitalize yourself...

YOUR CHOICE: ....

····························

THE PROCESS OF MANAGING PRIORITIES

····························

Our example demonstrates a global overhaul of the organizational system. For a lasting effect the following action needs to be taken:

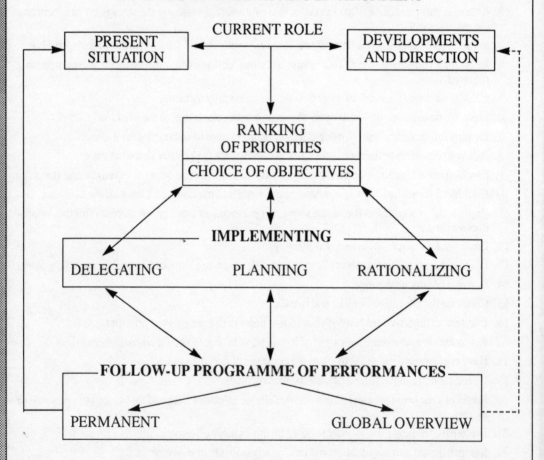

ANALYSIS OF THE EXISTING ENVIRONMENT

CURRENT ROLE

PRESENT SITUATION

DEVELOPMENTS AND DIRECTION

RANKING OF PRIORITIES
CHOICE OF OBJECTIVES

IMPLEMENTING

DELEGATING   PLANNING   RATIONALIZING

FOLLOW-UP PROGRAMME OF PERFORMANCES

PERMANENT   GLOBAL OVERVIEW

Follow these stages by examining, first of all, your present role under the headings *current situation* and *analysis of developments and direction*.

FROM REFLECTION TO ACTION

Peter Woods' situation may seem a bit of a caricature as it requires radical surgery rather than homeopathic treatment to put it right. However, it is not an isolated case: it brings to mind avalanche imagery – a situation can go downhill very rapidly. In a system of organization there exists a strong interaction between various activities. So, faced with a particularly stressful situation, a normally well-organized person could perhaps neglect what is usually their forte: the quality of his filing, planning a duty roster, respecting deadlines... Progressively like an oil stain, disfunctioning spreads from one area to another...

Peter Woods cannot build anything solid without first undertaking a complete reappraisal of his system of organization. This evaluation involves an analysis of the present situation (strengths/ weaknesses) while bearing in mind the future outlook (opportunities/ risks).

This approach must be global and detailed. It puts forward a broad overview but also meticulously directs certain key aspects of this functioning. This analysis should bring Peter Woods a balanced awareness of the present situation and also develop his motivation to act. You always feel better armed when you understand a situation...

Peter Woods undergoes a procedure which we are going to follow stage by stage. The results he obtained show the influence that each one of us can exert over his own organization and that of others. The first victory lies in convincing ourselves of this. Today, Peter Woods thinks in positive terms: he experiences a sense of satisfaction in his successes, he finds the time for exterior activities and now his contact with his team has increased so that there is a feeling of working together.

There is no great secret, simply a strong dose of lucidity and sacrifice: nothing gets solved by magic. This lucidity is achieved by separating ideal situations from objectives to be reached. It would be unrealistic to want to change all work methods and habits too quickly. You have to really work at realizing the objectives for the medium and short terms while respecting a realistic rhythm of transformation. In such a process of change you can't afford to burn all your boats.

THE CURRENT SITUATION

History is constantly repeating itself... Looking at your current practices, what are the five areas which you wish to analyse critically?

PROFESSIONAL SETTING

- ❏ Availability of facilities
- ❏ Coordination with associates
- ❏ Quality of group work
- ❏ Clarification of work requirements
- ❏ Awareness of forthcoming needs
- ❏ Strength of proposals
- ❏ Definition of who does what
- ❏ Working atmosphere
- ❏ ....

WORK METHODS

- ❏ Arranging appointments
- ❏ Decision making
- ❏ Problem analysis
- ❏ Follow-up and checking
- ❏ Processing correspondence
- ❏ Simplifying duties
- ❏ Unnecessary activities
- ❏ Work scheduling
- ❏ ....

MEANS AND EQUIPMENT

- ❏ Using the phone/fax
- ❏ Computer skills
- ❏ Quality of information
- ❏ Obstacles/working conditions
- ❏ Effective training
- ❏ Validity of statistics
- ❏ Delegation/autonomy
- ❏ Logistics
- ❏ Organization of available space
- ❏ ....

SKILLS AND BEHAVIOUR

- ❏ Listening attentively
- ❏ Respecting procedures
- ❏ Technical skills
- ❏ Negotiation
- ❏ Innovation/creativity
- ❏ Adapting to change
- ❏ Written expression
- ❏ Conducting meetings
- ❏ Classifying/filing
- ❏ ....

FROM THE PRIORITY CONCERNS OF THE COMPANY TO THE SPECIFICS OF YOUR ROLE

By looking at the developments in the professional environment and the strategy of the company, the priorities of your role can be verified. Know how to identify the link in the chain between the expectations of your superiors and the key directions of the company...

Your company
With regard to policy and anticipated actions for the coming period (6/12 months) write down in order of importance the three key concerns of your company: development, quality, profitability, redeployment of staff...

1 - ....

2 - ....

3 - ....

Your work unit
Taking into account the sector layout and the issues confronting your work unit (new equipment, skills to acquire, etc), outline carefully the three main concerns for the coming period:

1 - ....

2 - ....

3 - ....

Your role
With regard to the concerns of the unit, what for the same coming period, are the three priority expectations of your superiors vis-à-vis your role?

1 - ....

2 - ....

3 - ....

YOUR CURRENT ASSIGNMENT

At regular intervals (6/12 months), a clarification of your roles and responsibilities is essential. This procedure serves, in a dynamic way, to highlight your place and value in the current scheme of organization.

This clarification of the CURRENT ASSIGNMENT is the combination of the information collected in the three directions already mentioned: present situation, concerns of the company and of superiors, technical and organizational developments for the coming period.

This formalization of the CURRENT ASSIGNMENT is the first step towards the ranking of priorities. It concentrates on the essential and summarizes in a few lines (5-8) the purposes of a role. This is expressed in terms of objectives to be reached: maintaining the profitability of activities X and Y, improving the quality of the phone system, etc. The content should focus on the coming period (6-12 months), and on your specific contribution (factors considered as genuinely influential...).

Your current assignment

Section 2
OBJECTIVE ANALYSIS OF THE WORKLOAD

> *'Those who use their time badly are always the first to complain of its brevity.'*

Clarifying your current assignment is the first step towards defining priorities. It serves to reduce the influence of the urgent and an excessive dependence on immediate events. By itself it cannot help to distinguish priority matters from those which are not. In real terms this approach is insufficient to deal with the build-up caused by the unforeseen. Our perception of time is subjective, so we can't afford to skimp on an analysis of our workload. To do this we must critically examine our timetables and the position we take when faced with different tasks. We all know the consequences of underestimating the workload and the fate of certain tasks which in an overload situation are cancelled at the last minute, deferred or delegated under the worst conditions.

Managing our priorities calls for advance knowledge of the workload to allow us to appraise the practicality of projects and simplify decision-making.

We also have to allow for the unforeseen but we all know that efficiency depends in the main on the quality of our choices. In certain circumstances, we can be our own worst enemies. This is why it's worthwhile examining the workload as much in terms of quality as quantity. Analysis is really the best method of counteracting subjectivity when looking at the way we use our time.

The weekly or monthly review meeting is a common event within companies, but such an exercise often loses its value as it is not perceived positively by the parties concerned. Petty manipulations discredit any conclusions which may emerge. We are all aware of the difficulties involved in trying to reconstitute a timetable at the end of the day; you can depend on the fact that there will be wide disparities between what was planned and the reality of what was achieved.

We are all prisoners of our own habits. This situation is evident in the idiosyncrasies which make up our personalities, such as the need to check absolutely everything, a lack of thoroughness or perfectionism. When we're enjoying ourselves we lose track of time. In the same way, duties which are viewed as unattractive are sorted into the rejects pile to be dealt with 'later'. This results in the build-up of a backlog.

INVENTORY OF TASKS
EXERCISING PARASITIC INFLUENCE

Our advice is to list your favourite tasks as well as those you dislike. In so doing this reality becomes more objective. The findings could be important for the organization of your priorities.

ATTRACTIVE TASKS	UNATTRACTIVE TASKS
1.	1.
2.	2.
3.	3.
4.	4.
5.	5.

In the same way, it seems a useful exercise to identify those tasks regarded as simple or complex. In the general run of things it is quite possible that you prioritize the former to the detriment of the latter without due acknowledgement of their level of importance.

SIMPLE TASKS	COMPLEX TASKS
1.	1.
2.	2.
3.	3.
4.	4.
5.	5.

CONDUCTING AN ASSESSMENT OF YOUR WORKLOAD

Following on from a *qualitative* analysis, now undertake a *quantitative* analysis of your workload by filling in the table on the opposite page. The breakdown of your activity in percentage of time is calculated on a daily, weekly or monthly basis. The time framework can be defined in relation to the frequency and variety of tasks accomplished. A receptionist could obtain a satisfactory estimate by reasoning over the period of one day. A manager will probably have to settle on a monthly basis in order to cover all aspects of her role.

If you don't have sufficient information available on your timetable, you could organize a checklist. Collecting data in this way compiles a step-by-step databank. Gathering information as you go is the most complete but also the most restrictive method. For this reason use a less fussy procedure: at a given time, take stock of the past hour's schedule. Such an estimate over three or four days allows you to sort out the major trends of your professional activity. On reading the results, you can make adjustments to your estimate and increase the validity and accuracy of the estimate obtained.

An information databank may be drawn up and used according to your needs. As an illustration we've drawn up a frequently used model:

Time	Tasks Completed	Initiated		Planned		Observations
		Yes	No	Yes	No	

LIST OF PRINCIPAL TASKS

To gain a complete insight into your present organizational structure, list (starting with the highest) those tasks to which you currently devote the most time:

ORDER	DESCRIPTION OF TASK	PERCENTAGE OF TIME
1		
2		
3		
4		
5		
6		
7		
8		
9		
10		
11		
12		
13		
14		
15		
16		
17		
18		
19		
20		

ANALYSIS STAGE 1

An analysis of your checklists may throw light on some interesting aspects: on the overall volume of planned or unanticipated tasks, on the frequency or amount of time devoted to such and such a task...

But the main value of such an analysis lies in constructing a composite picture of your schedule in order to appreciate the significance of your main activities. Such a picture prevents the hazard of a too fragmented analysis where we get bogged down by detail and become incapable of a global judgement.

A sound approach permits us to group the entire body of tasks into ten main areas. As an example here is the analysis chart of a commercial assistant.

Such a regrouping allows us to assess our time structure at work and re-orientate certain aspects of our work organization. A commercial assistant could examine the balance of commercial/administrative time, prospecting/repeat selling time, and even time spent in/out of the office.

You must remember that management of priorities comes within the scope of a closed system as time is a limited commodity. When you over-invest in one area it is most certainly to the detriment of another...

FUNCTION OF A COMMERCIAL ASSISTANT

DESCRIPTION OF TASK	% TIME SPENT	% TIME DESIRED
1. Contact with prospective clients		
2. Travelling		
3. Customer contact		
4. Preparing meetings		
5. Compiling reports		
6. Administrative follow-up		
7. Team support		
8. Information/training		
9. Internal coordination		
10. Miscellaneous		
	100%	100%

Using a similar approach, now plan the analysis chart which corresponds best to the specifics of your job/role.

ANALYSIS STAGE 2

A second stage of analysis allows you to dissect your organizational style. It involves checking the amount of time devoted to different modes of action: PLANNING, ACTION, CHECKING, REACTION...

Are you more reactive or active?...

Does your system favour a preventative or curative approach?...

Is there a discrepancy between your intentions and your practices?...

In the same way it is interesting to analyse whether the timetable is conceived for the short or medium term. This means examining if the impact of each task has an immediate effect or one over a longer period. Each task does not have the same target: tidying your office is aimed at the very short term while the reorganization of records may have repercussions for activities over several months. Some tasks are more difficult to analyse. For instance, an initial meeting or interview with a client. Depending on the potential recognized, it could generate consequences over a day, a week... a year and longer...

Is your schedule more focused on results in the short term or the medium term? Consider your present assignment. Does the balance obtained seem to you satisfactory for the coming period?... If not, what changes do you envisage?...

FINDINGS

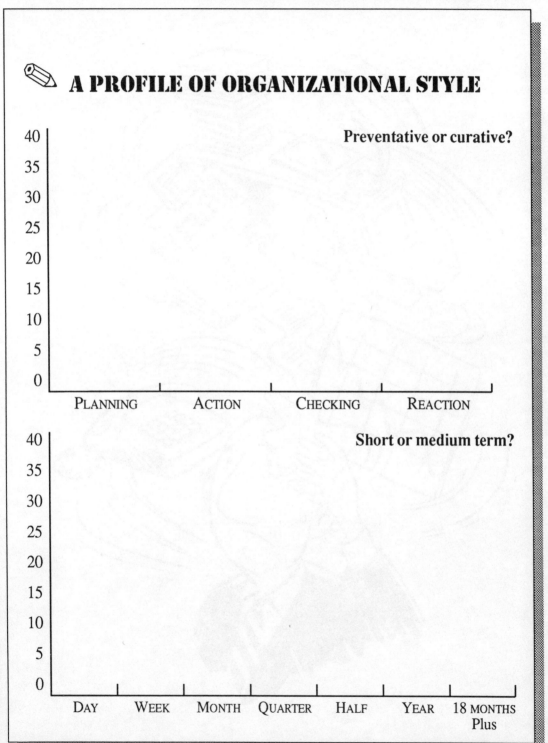

A PROFILE OF ORGANIZATIONAL STYLE

Preventative or curative?

40
35
30
25
20
15
10
5
0

PLANNING   ACTION   CHECKING   REACTION

Short or medium term?

40
35
30
25
20
15
10
5
0

DAY   WEEK   MONTH   QUARTER   HALF   YEAR   18 MONTHS Plus

Section 3
PRIORITIZING TASKS

> *'In the choice of priorities, the most difficult thing is to define the non-priorities...'*

Clarifying the current assignment and having a ready evaluation of the workload are the two essential prerequisites to prioritizing tasks. The first serves as a briefing on the role while the second specifies the method.

The next step is the process of prioritizing tasks, which is a major step towards the setting of operational objectives. It's a primary filter which acts by dividing tasks into two categories:

- priority tasks which have significant value and are deserving of special protection within the organizational framework...
- non-priority tasks which, without being sacrificed exactly, will occupy a more secondary or even marginal position...

Prioritizing tasks should be closely linked to the setting up of operational objectives. Together they make up the 'strategy' inspiring the tactical approach to daily situations. The 'setting of objectives' stage acts as a second filter and aims to accurately define the main results which need to be achieved. This, we can say, sifts out the top layer of priorities.

This dual exercise which distinguishes priority tasks from non-priority tasks may appear outmoded; however, it lies at the heart of our difficulties with both individual and collective organizations...

A PREVENTATIVE APPROACH

We have to move away from the style of management which goes with the flow, and chooses priorities on a short-term scale. If, in the thick of things, the system of prioritizing is not clear then we run the risk of seeing non-essential tasks taking a place they don't deserve.

Prioritizing tasks is a difficult procedure as our view of things seems to waver between the feeling that everything is done by intuition and the personal conviction that priorities within a role cannot be changed. There are those of us who adopt a system of constant improvisation (reactors) and those who respect, and sometimes cling to, tradition. These two sets of logic do not lead to a preventative approach.

It is probably true that the person occupying a particular post is best equipped to successfully instigate the procedure of prioritizing. The boss lacks sufficient information to carry through such a classification successfully. However, he needs to define concerns and objectives clearly in order to make it easier for the employee to prioritize.

To establish stability in your system of organization you need to reason it out over a 6 – 12 month period. Resist challenging this system on the slightest pretext and accept that adjustments can be made to increase efficiency later. There lies the difference between prioritization and choice of priorities. Our thinking relies on the significance of each task with regard to the current assignment. In work situations it will then be necessary to add to this the dimension of urgency.

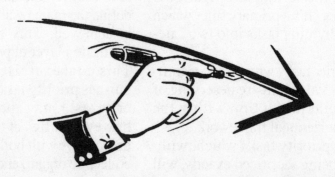

CAN YOU PRIORITIZE?

STATEMENTS	YES	NO
1. In a work situation you can easily classify the important tasks.		
2. There is no direct relation between your priorities and the amount of time you allocate to them.		
3. At the start of a month or week, priority activities are the subject of planning (day concerned, timetable slot...)		
4. You know for the coming period (6 – 12 months) the 20 per cent of tasks which represent 80 per cent of your added value to the company.		
5. Prioritizing tasks seems to you a false problem, given that in the same post, they are similar from one year to the next.		
6. Negotiating the priorities of your function with management is of limited benefit.		
7. By means of an objective analysis, you write, as soon as is necessary, a list and order of your priorities.		
8. Prioritizing tasks is a pointless exercise given that situations can develop so quickly.		
9. Priorities should be clearly defined by the management body.		
10. Today's priorities are never tommorrow's.		

If you answer NO to statements 1, 2, 3, 4, 7, 9, and 10 and YES to 5, 6, and 8, then this section should be particularly significant for you.

THE DEGREE OF IMPORTANCE APPROACH

All tasks do not have the same impact on the way a role is carried out. We must overcome the obstacle of looking at a job as a whole and attempt to break down the different aspects of a professional activity. As an analogy remember that in the education system some subjects are worth more than others. Depending on the career, maths carries more or less weight in the evaluation system while being associated with the goals projected.

In a professional environment, the assessment of a task's value should be made by the employee who carries it out. He determines his choices on the basis of his strengths/weaknesses and anticipated concerns and developments.

Evaluating the scale of importance of different tasks is a delicate exercise. Before going any further with it, have a look at the table below:

LEVEL	DEGREE OF IMPORTANCE	CHARACTERISTICS
A	ESSENTIAL	Strategic activity which in the current context claims particular attention. The stakes are high and it's imperative that it is accorded a top role in your schedule.
B	IMPORTANT	A compulsory part of your activity, this task cannot be overlooked because of the consequences implied.
C	FAIRLY IMPORTANT	Activity without any particular stakes. It should be handled within the scope of a fairly flexible programme with minimum concern.
D	SECONDARY	Marginal activity or one to be marginalized quickly. The attitude is to do nothing or delegate or pass on this task to someone else.

PRACTICAL EXERCISE

Before applying this evaluation table to your list of priorities, we suggest a spot of practice. Look at your current assignment and define the degree of importance (A,B,C,D) of each of these professional situations:

1. Regularly organizing your personal files and documentation (removing, cataloguing, amending…)

2. Taking care of a colleague's request. He has to solve a problem which he feels is delicate and calls upon your skills.

3. Identifying problems at large in the service in order to identify priority actions.

4. Reading correspondence in order to keep up to date with current news and events.

5. Holding frequent talks with superiors to draft an assessment and clarify the features in line for improvement in your organizational system.

6. Communicating with neighbouring services to establish a climate of cooperation.

7. Taking an active role at the heart of your team in the integration of new employees.

8. Bringing a formal review of your activities and results to the attention of your superiors every month.

9. Clarifying work procedures so as to limit time-wasting.

10. Reading reviews and journals specializing in your field.

11. Establishing and maintaining cordial relations with the other members of your team.

12. Ensuring by means of training the transfer of your professional skills to other team members.

13. Visiting other units engaged in similar activities to compare and evaluate the organizational system in place.

14. Preparing carefully for internal meetings.

15. Lending a spontaneous helping hand when excess work loads cause delays in daily operations.

16. Making sure that regulations and procedures are respected within the service.

17. Being on the alert for competition and market developments.

18. Keeping an account of statistics and results obtained by the service.

19. Dealing with an unhappy client or customer.

20. Dealing with an irregularity which is more irritating and repetitive than costly.

On completion of this exercise, note your responses on the following chart:

LEVEL	A	B	C	D
TOTAL				

In examining a task we often underestimate its degree of importance. If your responses belong mostly to categories A and B then it's already evident that on paper your system of prioritizing tasks is difficult to justify. And even more so when you consider that this often coincides with an underestimation of the time necessary for carrying out these tasks.

All activities cannot be essential or important. We must not mistake dreams for reality. Otherwise we risk wasting time and energy in all directions and end up only doing things by half.

The degree of importance a task has is relative to other demands on the agenda. It is therefore subject to change. In a football team everyone defends and everyone attacks. But not with the same intensity. At the end of a match all players are not judged on the basis of the same criteria.

The degree of importance concept is based on one person having responsibility for a particular function. We must also remember that this evaluation is appropriate only for a specified period of time (6/12 months...).

TASKS IN ORDER OF IMPORTANCE

Look at your current assignment. Record your high profitability tasks (A,B) and those which do not currently belong to this category.

HIGH PROFITABILITY TASKS (Levels A and B)

TASKS	LEVEL	PERCENTAGE OF TIME

LOW PROFITABILITY TASKS (Levels C and D)

TASKS	LEVEL	PERCENTAGE OF TIME

VALIDATING THE RESULTING ORDER
OF IMPORTANCE

Cast a critical eye on the choices just made and calculate the percentage of time spend on these activities for each level (A,B,C and D). Trace the curve obtained on the graph given:

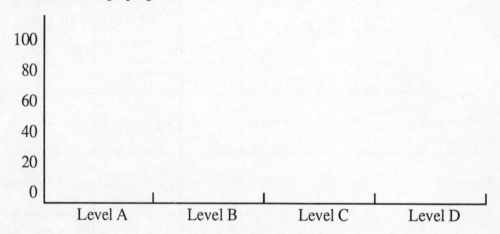

Compare the respective prominence of the different levels and the profile of your organizational system. What do you see? Does this priority ranking appear to be adapted to your needs and constraints?

Your remarks:

Prioritizing tasks is not easy. The right side of the chart always seems easier to fill in than the left. By using this approach we can understand our tendency to do non-priority tasks before priority ones. It is overload which jeopardizes. Knowing how to define your priorities puts you in the position of being able to identify the non-priorities. Ranking priorities brings us back to the theory of the domino effect. In desperate circumstances, we devote our complete attention to one task and this invariably takes time away from others. The worst solution is to spread ourselves too thinly. This absence of choice is equivalent to a partial commitment which is not a satisfactory solution to priority needs. Time is not elastic, we cannot postpone everything continually. We have to admit that we cannot be in two places at once. This logic implies that for lasting results we must, at certain times, commit ourselves to certain concerns. So, for the subsequent period, this ranking order could be subjected to serious modification. For example, we may wish to invest over a period of 6 – 12 months in in-house training (level A), then be content for the following period to benefit from this investment (level D). The choice of priorities takes into account the principle of cause and effect.

Interpretation of results

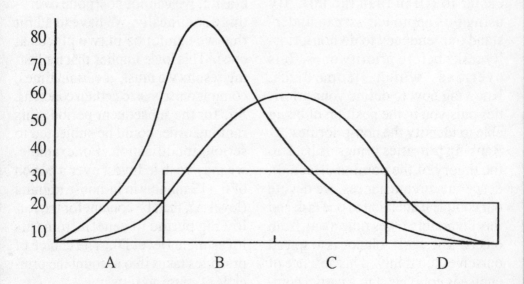

In normal management practice, the optimum conditions require a 50/50 division between high profitability tasks (A,B) and the rest. In a daily organization this reality offers the best guarantee of achieving the important and essential tasks in good conditions. Especially so for those responsibilities where trouble and the unforeseen frequently compromise planned progress. This situation with its opportunities for delegation and minimal investment allows greater flexibility in functioning. The essential activities (level 1) adhere to Pareto's law: *it's the 20 per cent of tasks which represent 80 per cent of the intrinsic value of your role.*

If your result does not correspond with this line of action, re-examine the definition of your current assignment and look again at the principal findings from your analysis of the present situation.

Section 4
OBJECTIVES AND ACTION PLAN

> *'If you don't know where to go, then any path can take you there...'*

Ranking priorities is a primary filter. It puts into perspective the prominence of the different tasks, and provides a concrete response to the demands of a job/function for a specified period.

Setting operational objectives refines this procedure by clarifying the results to be attained in the short and medium terms (3 – 12 months).

This choice of objectives is therefore a logical progression from the ranking of priorities. They will be chosen from the list of high profitability tasks. These are tasks which have particularly high stakes or a volume of work which is delicate to manage in the framework of the overall load.

This flash of insight into certain key aspects develops an added awareness and the motivation to act.

Setting yourself operational objectives and detailing a subsequent plan of action is the first phase of action.

OBJECTIVES TO GUIDE THE ACTION

ASSIGNMENTS, PRIORITIES and OBJECTIVES are the three areas for strategic consideration. Without a strategy there can be no effective tactic.

Fixing operational objectives is the result of the process which began with an assessment of the concerns and developments of the role.

In his book *Looking For Lost Time*, Alec MacKenzie, a leading authority on personal organization, puts forward the view that confused and changing priorities represent the primary cause of inefficiency.

If we are to attain success, there is no place for half measures or the unfinished. We must aim to render an objective stimulating, justifiable, realistic and ecologically sound. The chosen objectives must not subsequently be challenged without serious motives to justify such a decision.

The professional environment plays an essential role in success. The acceptance of our organizational system rests on the clarity of our objectives and a willingness to keep everyone concerned constantly informed. We should seek out allies: it is not possible to organize objectives effectively without the help and support of those around us.

PLANNING FOR THE FUTURE

Reasoning in terms of objectives is not usual practice in companies. We tend to use this technique for the big occasions: annual planning meetings, drawing up a schedule of conditions, individual assessments, etc.

It has little influence on daily functioning. This is regrettable as many actions would gain impact if, at the outset, the goal was clearly defined. Especially so in the case of studying a particular file, conducting an interview, purchasing material...

This procedure is not habitual so it is not perceived as normal. The problems involved are as much to do with psychology as method. It may be, for example, unwillingness to commit yourself to a particular contract or an inability to think ahead that makes prioritizing difficult. It is also the unease brought about by giving up the certainty of your present situation for the uncertainty of a new one.

CAN YOU SET YOUR OBJECTIVES?

STATEMENTS	YES	NO
1. You have no problem projecting into the future: 6 months, a year or more.		
2. For the coming 6 months, you know precisely the objectives to be reached.		
3. Your objectives are calculated on the basis of quantity, quality, costs, deadlines.		
4. Your objectives work as motivators.		
5. You're uncomfortable about translating objectives into concrete action.		
6. Your line of thinking is such that you always consider how to take action before clearly outlining the goal to be achieved.		
7. Reasoning in terms of objectives is the norm for you: decision to be taken, meeting to be held, problems to be solved.		
8. Objectives form part of your working professional practice, as both reference points and a means of negotiation.		
9. Writing out objectives is a pointless exercise.		
10. Keeping track of developments demands frequent modification of the level of precision expected.		
TOTAL		

Your knowledge of the subject is fine if your answers are positive for statements 1,2,3,4,7,8 and negative for the rest.

Your Situation:

Can you accurately recall an event which happened around 6 months ago?

Going back further in time, can you recall something that happened this time last year?

Would you be capable of accurately retracing the main achievements of your programme for the last three days?

In the same way, is next week's programme clearly engraved on your mind?

On a professional level, can you visualize the transformation or development of your role in the coming year?

Would you be capable of indicating what will become of your professional responsibilities in the next two to three years?

HOW DO YOU RELATE TO TIME?

One thing is obvious: in this exercise certain people will find it easier to position themselves in the past, others in the future.

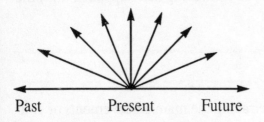

Past   Present   Future

What is your position? Are you centred more in the PAST? PRESENT? FUTURE? No doubt this profile greatly influences your style of organization. The way we relate to time influences our perception of events. Are we going to be sensitive to the historical background of a situation or to its potential developments? Are we going to carry out our tasks because of the mood of the moment? So the exercise of setting objectives does not depend solely on organizational climate. It touches also on certain psychological aspects of the individual and on his capacity to think ahead to the future.

At this point it is interesting to identify what your position is on the time line. Ask yourself the questions on page 41. Do you feel that you stand outside or in contact with this line?

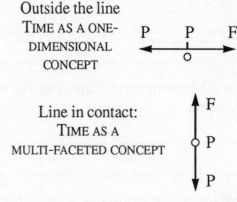

Outside the line
TIME AS A ONE-
DIMENSIONAL
CONCEPT

Line in contact:
TIME AS A
MULTI-FACETED CONCEPT

POSITIONING ON THE TIME LINE

In the first example, time only has one dimension: it is seen as a tangible reality. Standing outside the line allows us to stand back and make a concrete evaluation of the situation. Time is organized into distinct sequences; it can be broken down. This approach favours planning as we can look at doing one thing at a time. There is frequent reference to objectives.

In the second example, time is multifaceted and knows no limits. Time is adjustable. There is less of an opportunity to distance ourselves and it is more difficult to make choices. We often do several things at once.

SETTING OPERATIONAL OBJECTIVES

In direct relation to the analysis conducted in the section 'prioritizing tasks', now list your operational objectives. In order to focus your energies on the essential, limit yourself to a total of 5:

OPERATIONAL OBJECTIVES	DEADLINES FORECAST
1.	
2.	
3.	
4.	
5.	

Now look critically at the formulation of your objectives.

Planning is a far less inherent aspect than in the other system and reference to objectives is not really developed.

Being aware of these elements helps us to take the active measures necessary to succeed in setting up operational objectives.

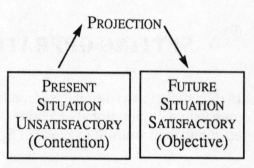

Now remind yourself of the four qualities of an operational objective: it must be *stimulating*, *justifiable*, *realistic* and *in keeping with the work environment*.

DEFINITION AND CHARACTERISTICS OF AN OPERATIONAL OBJECTIVE

Definition: *an operational objective may be defined as the solid and measurable result set for achievement in a given period of time through appropriate action.*

Setting objectives is essential to prioritizing successfully. First you identify the goal to be achieved, then you identify the means and solutions which subsequently ensure that it is achieved in practice. It is a case of not 'putting the cart before the horse'. Instead of thinking in terms of training, which is only a means to an end, we look at what we hope to achieve by it: have we the capacity and variety of skills among members of the team?

IS THE OBJECTIVE STIMULATING?

There is nothing more motivating than an objective once certain conditions are met. These involve both the formulation and the content.

Formulation: An objective must be expressed in positive terms if it is to be stimulating. Our brains are not equipped to tune into the negative. It is far better to identify the goal to be aimed at than the result to be avoided.

'Not to smoke any more' is not a stimulating objective. By expressing it in this way the inherent risk is of reinforcing the desire to smoke rather than overcoming it. The objective should express the expected result in terms of the positive benefits of the future situation.

Example: *To participate in a mini-marathon.*

The content: the content of an objective should be stimulating. The objective should conform to the individual's beliefs and values. It is difficult to get excited about a result if your involvement is only skin-deep. Convictions cannot be negotiated. If you are not personally convinced of the importance of running this mini-marathon then it means that the objective is irrelevant or premature.

STATEMENTS AND MODIFICATIONS:

CAN THE OBJECTIVE BE JUSTIFIED?

This question addresses the way in which you could verify the achievement of the objective. It is always difficult to evaluate your own performances. In forming an objective you must, from the outset, make the job of the final evaluation easier.

The deadline: a first necessity is to decide on a completion date. This covers the period for realization of the goal or the checking of its actual effectiveness.

Example: *15/04: Establish an action plan to reorganize business records. 30/08: Systematic employment of commercial records according to the procedure defined on the 31/01.*

A specific result: the evaluation forecast at the completion date justifies a totally unambiguous assessment of the result obtained. The result should be decisive. Either the objective is reached or it is not.

Example: *on 30/06 the accuracy of the business records should reach 80 per cent of the total information defined in the contract.*

An accurate assessment always makes the achievement of the objective easier. If there remains any doubt you would be well advised to verify the clarity of the objective through a third party.

STATEMENTS AND MODIFICATIONS:

~~~~~~~~~~~~~~~~~~~~~~~~~~~~~~~~~~

~~~~~~~~~~~~~~~~~~~~~~~~~~~~~~~~~~

~~~~~~~~~~~~~~~~~~~~~~~~~~~~~~~~~~

~~~~~~~~~~~~~~~~~~~~~~~~~~~~~~~~~~

~~~~~~~~~~~~~~~~~~~~~~~~~~~~~~~~~~

~~~~~~~~~~~~~~~~~~~~~~~~~~~~~~~~~~

IS THE OBJECTIVE REALISTIC?

We must, of course, be realistic when forming our objectives. The difficulty of our approach rests on this dilemma: an objective should be at once ambitious and accessible.

The power: this hinges on the potential for action and influence the person concerned thinks he or she wields. It is essential that they are convinced of their ability to act. Of course the result still remains a fragile thing to attain but the means and resources available demonstrate the feasibility of the operation. There are many ways to get to Rome but it is necessary that all your plans are workable.

Example: *to achieve 80 per cent accuracy in business records I will be able to draw on X's advice, and through a study be able to pick out the main problem areas or even benefit from...*

The time available: the feasibility of the objective may be challenged by the deadline imposed on the project. In fact, our natural tendency is to underestimate the amount of time necessary to carry out a task.

The objective will be outlined as a set of intermediary objectives if the deadline seems too distant.

PROCESS OF VALIDATION

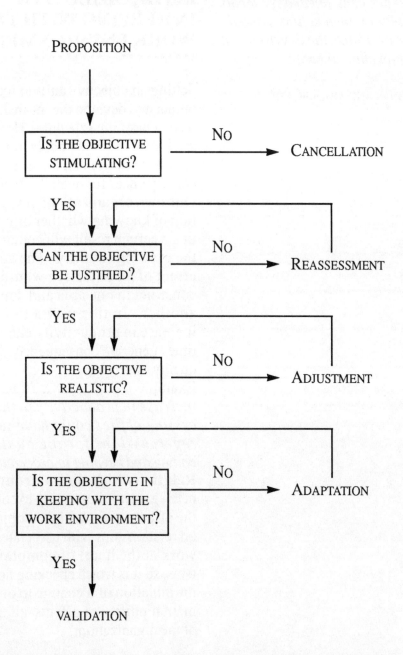

PROPOSITION

IS THE OBJECTIVE STIMULATING? — NO → CANCELLATION

YES

CAN THE OBJECTIVE BE JUSTIFIED? — NO → REASSESSMENT

YES

IS THE OBJECTIVE REALISTIC? — NO → ADJUSTMENT

YES

IS THE OBJECTIVE IN KEEPING WITH THE WORK ENVIRONMENT? — NO → ADAPTATION

YES

VALIDATION

Example: *if it seems that '30/04, to attain 80 per cent accuracy' seems over ambitious, then at first we could envisage on 15/02, the development of an action plan...then...*

STATEMENTS AND MODIFICATIONS:

••••••••••••••••••••••••••••

IS THE OBJECTIVE IN KEEPING WITH THE WORK ENVIRONMENT?

••••••••••••••••••••••••••••

Setting an objective aims to increase output and develop the intrinsic merits of a working schedule. However, we know that emphasizing a few specific results can have negative consequences for overall efficiency.

Our own organization: it is a question of knowing whether or not getting a certain result will compromise the existing stability. The adverse effect of an objective would be to construct in one area and demolish another. In this way a too rapid increase in productivity can sometimes generate consequences for the quality of service.

Example: *aiming for a 20 per cent increase in productivity in the processing of files could have serious repercussions for the quality of coding and keeping to procedures.*

Relations with the environment: here again it is interesting to consider the effects of an achieved objective on relationships with associates. We work at the heart of complex systems, so it is worth checking how the introduction of a change to one element modifies or affects all or part of the organization.

Beyond pinpointing any possible adverse effects, the aim of this is to round off the process of adapting the objective.

By exercising our critical faculties before taking action, we increase our determination to act once the objective is justified.

STATEMENTS AND MODIFICATIONS:

DEVELOPMENT OF A PERSONAL ACTION PLAN

Defining operational objectives clarifies what we want to achieve in the coming months. To round off this exercise we need to identify the actions which work towards their productive functioning.

The Personal Action Plan (PAP) is a way of doing the spadework. It doesn't pretend to go into detail or offer a guarantee of success. In practice, things often turn out to be either simpler or more difficult than expected.

In any event realizing an objective is a complex operation. Several actions are necessary and their synchronization and timing are often the difference between success or failure. However, the interesting aspect of such a procedure is that by setting out the steps to be taken or stages, we demystify the goal to be reached. Tom Thumb dotted the path he was taking with small stones. In a forward looking perspective why not derive inspiration from such an approach? When we know the road it is always easier to travel. Most action plans are doubtless worked out in an informal way. A written formalization of the plan permits a deeper analysis, and usually produces a greater return on the interaction of the various elements involved.

Draw up an action plan based on one of your objectives to achieve maximum impact.

THE IMPLEMENTATION OF AN OPERATIONAL OBJECTIVE

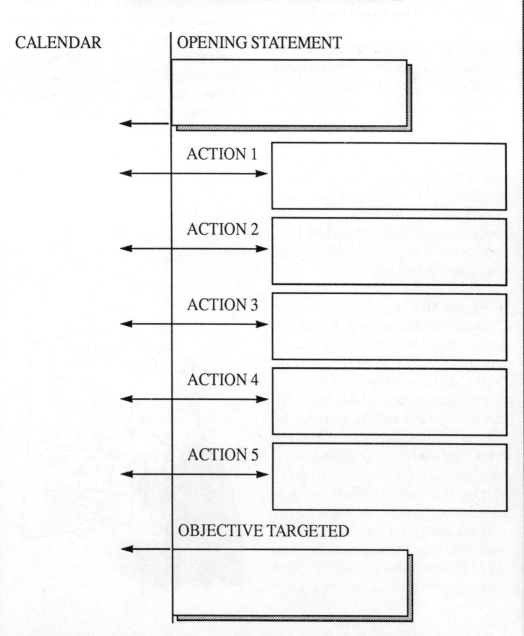

CALENDAR

OPENING STATEMENT

ACTION 1

ACTION 2

ACTION 3

ACTION 4

ACTION 5

OBJECTIVE TARGETED

METHODS OF PROGRAMMING

Defining our objectives is a way of providing ourselves with a strategy for change. The action plan illustrates the programme of actions necessary to the achievement of objectives. These actions are intended to revitalize the existing situation, either by improving reported inadequacies, or by adapting to known or anticipated developments.

Once the goal is clearly identified, two methods of programming action plans can be envisaged:

1. Retroactive method

This method works on a countdown basis. Following on from the clarification of the goal to be reached (on 30/09, to obtain 95 per cent accuracy in the updating of business records), the method consists of tracing the operation backwards. We move from the final situation to the initial one, pinpointing the intermediary stages: if I want to fulfil this objective, I must first of all obtain 92 per cent accuracy over three months, but to do that I need to improve the quality of existing files by checking that each one provides the required information.

2. Proactive method

The proactive method proceeds in chronological order. After the preliminary clarification of goals, it continues by defining the programme stage by stage. The starting point is the initial stage and we end with the final one. In the example, the action plans could include:
– choosing a team,
– identifying principal causes,
– proposing an improvement plan.

SCHEDULING EXERCISES

Decide on the technique you wish to follow then do the following exercises:

SITUATION: *the project for the weekend is to repaint your bedroom. Consider all the clutter and work involved. You want to be completely finished by Sunday evening. Use the retroactive method to draw up your work programme:*

PRESENT SITUATION A	4	3	2	1	FUTURE SITUATION B

1. ....

2. ....

3. ....

4. ....

SITUATION: *you've made your decision. This year you're going to celebrate your birthday with a party for 50 guests. You've got a month, and everything to do as you don't have access to a place big enough to hold that number of people. Use the proactive method to draw up your work programme:*

PRESENT SITUATION A	1	2	3	4	FUTURE SITUATION B

1. ....

2. ....

3. ....

4. ....

CONSTRUCT YOUR PERSONAL ACTION PLAN

The role of an action plan is to lay out the conditions of success, to verify the validity of procedures selected for each objective and to calculate the corresponding measures.

INSTRUCTIONS:
1. Make a thorough list of actions to be performed, either using the proactive method (from the initial to the final stage) or the opposite retroactive method (work backwards from the objective to the present situation). In the case of complex objectives we recommend the second method.

2. Arrange your list of actions in chronological order and estimate the length of time needed to carry them out. If the estimate is finely balanced, use this method:

$$\frac{\text{Minimum time} + \text{maximum time} + 4 \times \text{probable time}}{6}$$

3. Starting with the deadline, work out the amount of time expected for each stage. It is usually better to overestimate the time necessary. Example: *if 1.5 days seems necessary to you, then choose a period 02/04 – 07/04 in order to take into account possible distractions or other demands on your time.*

4. Verify the overall coherence of your action plan (significance of each stage, feasibility, etc) and establish at this point which are the principal and/or delicate stages.

PERSONAL ACTION PLAN

OBJECTIVE:

No	ACTIONS TO TAKE	OVERALL DURATION	BEGINNING	END
1				
2				
3				
4				
5				
6				
7				
8				
9				
10				

Section 5
BUILDING YOUR SYSTEM OF ORGANIZATION

'Nature abhors a vacuum...'

An efficient company builds its success on the choice of suitable objectives. It also draws on a stable system of organization which concerns in particular, work procedures and programmes of responsibility.

This statement can be verified on an individual plane. There can be no efficient management of priorities if it doesn't fall within the framework of a coherent system.

The system of organization responds to the following questions: What? How much? When? How? It gives us an overview of the workload, clarifies the level of responsibility for the tasks to be completed, the allocation of time, and the options available in economic planning.

Continuing the analogy with the management of a company, note the existence of 'fixed responsibilities' and 'variable responsibilities'. It is the same story in your own organizational system: a great number of tasks are known quantities, to calculate them doesn't require a crystal ball. Each week isn't fundamentally different from the preceding one. There are constants. Your workload is compiled of a 'hard core' of repetitive activities on which it is wise to check the efficiency and relevance of procedures at frequent intervals (6/12 months). This process aims at defining a blueprint timetable adapted to objectives and priorities.

DEFINING YOUR MODEL ORGANIZATION

Trying to define your model organization may appear paradoxical in an unsettled context. Taking such a precaution does, however, justify the disruption: it reduces stress levels and improves the speed of intervention. When faced with uncertainty we feel an increased need for points of reference even though we are aware that certain situations call for unforeseen options.

Do not imagine that this process will have the effect of extinguishing the capacity to adapt. Quite the opposite is true, the ability to react is strengthened. We can look at ice hockey to illustrate this point. Ice hockey is one of the fastest sports in the world. It calls on the most rigorous systems of organization. The thoroughness of this system develops the tactical intelligence of the players during play.

This system of organization must not become rigid. Its aim lies in providing modes of functioning which will be operative in 80 per cent of situations. Clarifying what the model organization should be reduces irrelevant actions and encourages regulation of the system.

ANALYSIS AND CHOICE OF FUNCTIONING MODES

The unforeseen is all too often a pretext for not organizing things that fall well within our range of capabilities. When we possess a real perspective of the workload involved, it would be a pity not to use such a means of decision making.

Make a chart and list all of the tasks included in your job/function. Take into account the following points:

1. *Clarify the degree of importance of each task* (for yourself, for the current period) using the following scale. A: essential, B: important, C: fairly important, D: secondary...

2. *Specify the level of responsibility*, in other words your position vis-à-vis each task. E: execution, A: assistance, C: coordination/control, S: Supervision...

3. *Give the name of the person who takes over the activity* when it seems necessary to you (taking into account previous responses) to distance yourself a little.

4. *Determine the frequency of assuming the task* (daily, weekly, monthly, immediately); a lot of time-wasting can be linked to a bad definition of time scale.

CAN YOU STRUCTURE YOUR SYSTEM OF ORGANIZATION?

STATEMENTS	YES	NO
1. Your colleagues feel that it is difficult to stand in for you in cases of absence or overload.		
2. Do you recognize those activities at risk, in other words, those which generate serious problems for your organizational system?		
3. Taking the workload into account, establishing the length of a delay is a sensitive exercise.		
4. You frequently challenge accepted appointment times or deadlines.		
5. The level of responsibility for your tasks is clear; this prevents doubling and time-wasting.		
6. You are happy with automatic procedures, while keeping an eye on their degree of efficiency.		
7. Investing in organization presents the disadvantage of making practices too rigid.		
8. You employ work procedures to complete long and complex tasks.		
9. Precision and adaptability don't go hand in hand.		
10. To invest too heavily in your own organizational system is to set yourself up for many disappointments.		
TOTAL		

If your responses to this questionnaire were **YES** for nos. 2,5,6,8 and **NO** for the others, then you will find confirmation of your practices in this section, and some ways to back them up more solidly.

5. *Define the average time investment required for each task*, while making sure that the overall volume is in line with the chosen methods. Calculating by the method on page 54 gives us a figure which is sufficiently precise.

6. *Plan as soon as it appears possible or desirable*, the most appropriate time-slot or period. The level of precision has to be defined according to the need and specifications of the task (frequency, degree of urgency, etc).

This covers rigid planning (Wednesday morning 10 – 12, the last Friday afternoon of the month 2 – 3 o' clock...) and flexible scheduling (1st week of the month, every Tuesday, etc).

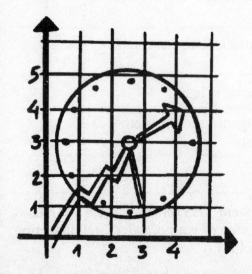

PRACTICALITY OF THE PROCESS

Is it really necessary to submit ourselves to such a complex process in order to obtain convincing results? The answer to this depends on the context of the specific task in hand. This decision to start from scratch with your work organisation has several aims.

1. **To evaluate the workload and validate the choice of operational objectives.** In effect, it will be possible to spot quickly if the amount of time available exceeds the time that the plan of action requires and whether it is compatible with the 'fixed responsibility' budget.

If not, it will be necessary to revise the goals or review the allocation of time for those tasks which are highly time-consuming.

2. **To identify those activities which are at risk and so ensure a follow-up that is better targeted.** If and when you experience difficulty in defining a task (frequency, average time needed to complete the task, etc) it is an indicator that this task is not under control. It is therefore a potential time-waster and must be supervised carefully. By correcting this, it will then be possible to get reliable information in the future.

ANALYSIS OF TASKS

TASKS	DEGREE OF IMPORT.	LEVEL OF RESPON.	DELEGATION	FREQUENCY	AVERAGE DURATION	(P) PLANNED (NP) NOT PLANNED	PLANNING		
							WEEK	DAY	TIME
<u>Management Administration</u>	C				30%				
-processing correspondence	D	S	Perrin						
-reading correspondence	C	C	Woods	day	15 mins	P			10-10.15
-drafting correspondence	B	E		day	30 mins	P			2-2.30
-monitoring programmes	C	C	Rogers	month	1 hour	P	2nd		
-customer claims	B	C	Woods	immediately	?	NP			
-account adjustments	C	C	Rogers	2 months	1 hour	P		15 - 30	afternoon
....									
<u>Informing/Training of Personnel</u>	A				8%				
-daily briefing	A	E		day	15 mins				9-9.15
-departmental meeting	A	E		weekly	1 hour	P	Thursday		10-10.30
....									

61

3. To balance the workload by the decisions taken and to develop the capacity for adaptation. The best form of guarantee for the protection of priorities and objectives comes from a flexible workload. Extremes should be avoided and a more synchronized timetable established. This involves balancing the workload as well as the sequence of events.

To make its implementation easier, the decisions taken can be examined on a reference sheet: THE THEORETICAL TIMETABLE (see opposite).

THE THEORETICAL TIMETABLE

The theoretical timetable is an important contribution to the system of organization you want to install. It forms the conclusion of a preliminary process and, in this way, it does not compete with the use of an agenda.

THE THEORETICAL TIMETABLE adds an overview to the agenda and a stability to the workload (the norms to be respected, favoured options). It offers a reference framework, and facilitates the planning of activities ensuring medium-term management.

It fulfils the double needs of anticipation and prevention.

USING AN AGENDA

THE AGENDA offers the theoretical timetable a partial but instant view of events. It allows for adaptation within the ground rules and for taking stock of opportunities. In its way it encourages periodical assessment and analysis of the difficulties experienced.

The purpose of a theoretical timetable

1. To visualise the overview of tasks to be accomplished in a single document.
2. To facilitate the agenda planning of infrequent tasks (spur of the moment) and so avoid omissions and extremes.
3. To place you in a position to draw up assessments (measure the gap between the planned/achieved, etc).
4. To pinpoint immediately the significant developments in the workload.

THEORETICAL TIMETABLE

Time	PLANNED DAILY AND WEEKLY ACTIVITIES					PLANNED WEEKLY AND MONTHLY ACTIVITIES				IMMEDIATE ACTIVITIES
	Monday	Tuesday	Wednesday	Thursday	Friday	Activities	Week	Day	Time	
8 am						Monitoring programme (1 hr)	2nd			Sorting correspondence
9			DAILY BRIEFING			Preparing departmental meeting 30 mins				Filing/records
10		READING CORRESPONDENCE (WITH WOODS)				Account adjustments (1 hr)		Wednesday	Afternoon	Inventory stocks and supplies
								15.30		
11				DEPT MEETING						Customer claims
12										
1 pm										
2			LUNCH							
		DRAFTING CORRESPONDENCE								
3										
4										
5										
6										

INTRODUCING A SYSTEM OF ORGANIZATION

The system of organization offers a framework of reference for every type of timetable. But this system goes beyond the options taken in terms of planning; it is concerned with the HOW of the action, that is to say, with the methods of work. Efficiency requires the acquisition of several reflex responses defined from a starting point of rational processes. Our ability to adapt depends as much on alertness to our environment (listening to needs, grabbing opportunities, etc) as on discipline shown (norms, regulations, etc) in regard to the situations most frequently encountered:

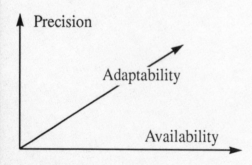

You cannot waste time every day on discovering the basics.

Adaptability is not simply a synonym for availability or lack of planning. You must arm yourself with work procedures which aim to optimize the time needed to execute repetitive operations: filing documents, reading instructions, analysing problems or conducting a meeting.

OPTIMIZING WORK METHODS

Every job/function presents its own specific characteristics and inefficiencies. Most methods become obsolete no matter what their initial value. We know that routine alters our judgement. When we see things too close at hand, we no longer manage to pick out weaknesses and time wasting. In order to optimize your work methods you should:
1. List the 10 most repetitive tasks in your timetable (reference to the analysis carried out on the workload in section 2 will help you here);
2. Do the evaluation for each of them in terms of the actual performance level. It corresponds to the cost-efficiency relationship, that is, the quality and productivity obtained in relation to the amount of time put in.

PERFORMANCE AND OPTIMIZATION
OF METHODS

Situations	Performance Level	Order of Priority
1.		
2.		
3.		
4.		
5.		
6.		
7.		
8.		
9.		
10.		

The optimizing of your methods may involve some time for reflection. If this is the case, don't forget to plan the necessary periods. Always bear in mind that it's more often 'economical' to draw on the ideas of other people in activities similar to your own, than to invent a new approach. Why re-invent the wheel?

This evaluation can be assessed in line with the following scale:

5 = excellent,
3 = satisfactory,
2 = insufficient,
1 = mediocre

3. Classify on a scale of 1 to 10 these different tasks in terms of how much time could be saved; in other words, in terms of return on investment.

Section 6
MANAGING DAILY SITUATIONS

Everyone agrees that efficient priority management demands determination, thoroughness and continuity. This may mean the introduction of a somewhat ruthless aspect to your system of organization. It is essential to avoid a situation where priority management is challenged by:
– numerous obstacles upsetting planned schedules and activities (postponements, delays, decisions put off until the last minute, lack of information, etc);
– countless requests where reflex wins over reflection, the effectiveness of a prompt result over the impact of change in the medium term, etc.
Managing priorities demands clear thinking and it is important not to rely just on instinct to detect essential concerns and objectives.
In a fast-moving routine where days follow one another but no two are alike, the meaning of our actions is not easy to pin down. This lends considerable weight to the argument that an evaluation of daily events is essential to the overall control of your schedule.

INTERESTING POINTS

The management of priorities is constantly evident in our capacity to face up to events. We immediately become aware of the following:
1. This approach rarely relies on a method which outlines the various aspects to be taken into consideration. Intuition tends to prevail over methodical analysis.
2. Recourse to a method never happens unless the situation appears particularly difficult to control.

Stress and objectivity are incompatible...

3. A lack of precision often sanctions the use of the criteria of urgency and importance: in a head to head situation the urgent always wins over the important.

4. The evaluation is too exclusively focused on the present (immediate action) without any real reference or regard for the past or future.

All these observations lead us to adopt a methodological approach to daily situations. To have any real effect this should become a consistent reflex.

• •
TACTICAL APPROACH TO A SITUATION
• •

The right relationship between choosing priorities and the ability to adapt where necessary is a prerequisite for efficiency. What upsets this balance is the speed with which we have to respond to different requests. This quality is called reactivity.

Being consistent and reactive demands a good balance of action and reflection. For this we must use a simple but productive line of questioning. This is the purpose of the optimization flow chart.

1. Is it worth acting upon? This question implies more than you may think. In some conflicts the best action is to do nothing. Experience proves that we often get bogged down with a host of mediocre activities such as reading internal memos or reviews surplus to our information needs.

2. Is it up to me to act? In the heat of the action, we often take on board tasks which are not strictly our own (from colleagues, associates, etc). We should refuse to get involved and/or pass them along to those responsible. In certain cases the task may be part of our job or function but given our choice of priorities we cannot assume responsibility for it. In such circumstances we should delegate immediately or temporarily.

3. Is it urgent that I act? We have a tendency either to underestimate the degree of urgency of a situation or be subjected to bogus urgency. Watch out for this and try to be precise and realistic about setting time limits. If it doesn't require immediate handling then take advantage of the flexibility this offers. Plan immediately so as not to forget.

OPTIMIZATION FLOW CHART

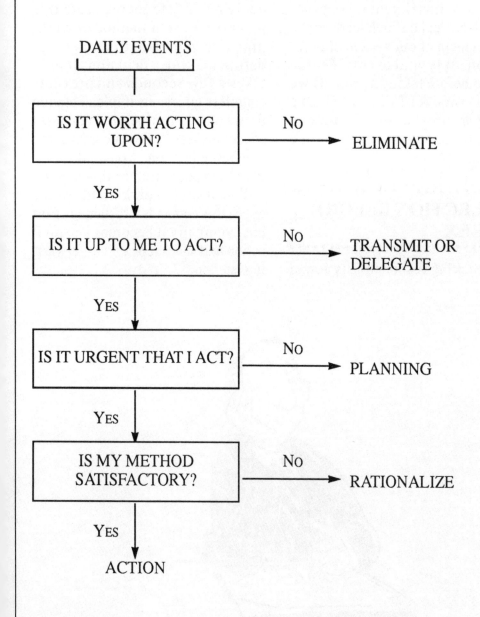

DAILY EVENTS

| IS IT WORTH ACTING UPON? | → No → | ELIMINATE |

Yes ↓

| IS IT UP TO ME TO ACT? | → No → | TRANSMIT OR DELEGATE |

Yes ↓

| IS IT URGENT THAT I ACT? | → No → | PLANNING |

Yes ↓

| IS MY METHOD SATISFACTORY? | → No → | RATIONALIZE |

Yes ↓

ACTION

4. Is my method satisfactory? Force of habit and impulse sometimes lead us to adopt inefficient work practices. A critical outlook leads to the improvement of our system of organization. It is vital to consider the method before taking action. If we lack the time for full analysis, we should ensure that we take time to review our methods and plans at a later date.

REFLECTION BEFORE REFLEX

Before taking responsibility for an action, take time to reflect and fully consider the implications of such a decision. Try to incorporate this process into your method of working. It is important to think twice before making a decision. It only takes a few seconds and prevents countless errors. Its implementation draws on a key principle: you must accept losing a little time in order to gain more later on. You could compare the acquisition of this method with learning to park a car. At the outset this demands a sustained effort but eventually it becomes a natural action and saves repeated time-wasting later on.

CAN YOU MANAGE DAILY SITUATIONS?

STATEMENTS	YES	NO
1. You never just skim through your correspondence before proceeding to a more detailed scrutiny.		
2. Concerned for quality, you always respond promptly to the request of a third party.		
3. Your workmates are ignorant of your procedure for dealing with correspondence.		
4. You have set up a filter system, effectively cutting down on disruptions such as visits and phone calls.		
5. Faced with a demand from your superiors, it always seems tricky to say no.		
6. During a chaotically busy period, you can take time out for reflection.		
7. Your definition of the word urgent is clear and precise.		
8. Before making a decision on a complex situation, you take the time to measure the impact of your decision for the medium term.		
9. Every morning you visualize the anticipated shape of your day on paper so as to absorb its restrictions and opportunities.		
10. Faced with an urgent request, you never hesitate about the method to use.		
TOTAL		

If your responses are positive for nos 4,6,7,8,9 and negative for the rest then your current method simplifies the evaluation of events.

EVALUATION OF EVENTS

Processing correspondence – what better exemplifies the management of daily situations? The quality of your working method generates repercussions for the whole of your organizational system. This task lies at the very heart of priority management. It is the ideal opportunity to highlight the strategy and options selected in advance. This is the occasion when the order of priorities is decided and the time limits and precautionary measures approved.

In order to avoid the stranglehold of routine, use a method to evaluate events which span four distinct viewpoints.

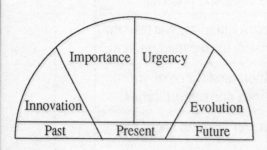

IMPORTANCE

Examine the degree of importance of an event and consider whether it is necessary to introduce a specific procedure for this situation. This decision should be based on what is at stake and the objectives you wish to achieve.

The importance of a task depends on:
– *your role,* in other words, the priorities you have fixed for the period in question.
– *the context of the action*, knowing the consequences of the situation.

It is necessary at this point to clarify the roles of everyone at the heart of the organization and the system of objectives pursued.

EXAMPLE
In your correspondence you discover a circular sent out by the Managing Director. He wants to reduce general expenditure. This circular requests that all constructive measures be taken to reduce the number of photocopies, phone calls and use of stationery.

In your opinion, is this situation:

❏ *important?*

❏ *not important?*

In a general climate of cutting back, this additional demand generates a particularly close interest. But we are likely to view the situation differently if steps have already been taken in this direction and have produced convincing results.

• •

URGENCY

• •

When considering the urgency factor of a task we are asking the question 'Does this need immediate handling?'. To answer this we must look at whether the task is based on the need for immediate action or in relation to a situation of necessity involving the safety and security of goods and people. The answer plays a major deciding role in the ranking of priorities. But the term 'urgent' is often abused. It is a safe bet that something will get done within a satisfactory time limit if it is labelled urgent. The urgency factor is relative to:
– *the time limit* imposed by your professional environment.
– *your capacity for immersion*. It is important to know how available you are within the set time limit, relative to the time necessary for completion of the activity.

Urgency requires reactivity and synchronization. It sometimes suffers from a certain lack of precision. Individuals have their own definition of urgency. Should we act at once? As soon as possible? Today? This all-purpose word creates a great deal of ambiguity. It is easier and more accurate to employ the definition of a specific time limit.

EXAMPLE
You find several departmental memos demanding an immediate response. This is a difficult situation as you will have to defer important business. Your hesitation is increased because you suspect your associates of making unjustifiable demands.

In your opinion is this situation:

❏ *urgent?*

❏ *non-urgent*

It is almost impossible to determine the difference between real or fake urgencies.
This makes it essential to clarify the rules of the game in advance, otherwise associates are going to encounter serious coordination difficulties in the future. In effect, if everything becomes urgent then nothing really is so.

INNOVATION

When we examine the innovative aspect of an event we must ask the question, 'Are we confronted here with a new situation or the usual kind of thing?' Our judgement is based on how often a case like this crops up and the amount of experience we may or may not have for finding a solution to it.

This approach allows us to make a permanent diagnosis of our practices. As well as helping to identify a new situation, it allows you to cast a critical eye over your work methods. Innovation is relative to:

– *whether or not there is a set organizational system* in place to deal with the event, and procedures favouring its effective completion.

– *the results gained* beforehand given the means and restrictions available.

In effect, if the handling of a repeated activity is unsatisfactory this approach is extremely useful. It points to a need for the situation to become innovative. A work procedure is established for the job. This can then become obsolete in the light of further developments.

EXAMPLE
You discover among your correspondence a request for information from a client. This reminds you of two similar cases one of which turned up only a few hours ago. Nothing has yet been laid down in the group's organization for managing such situations which makes for lost time.

In your opinion, is this situation:

❑ *innovative?*

❑ *not innovative?*

Some one-off tasks arise which present no great cause for concern. They are dealt with and no one pays them any further attention. They can, however, generate all kinds of anomalies and chaos. Keeping an eye on the innovation of our systems helps us to remain wary of the influence of force of habit in our working methods. At the same time we can oversee the consolidation of an organizational system.

EVOLUTION

Looking at the evolution of an event is one way of approaching the question, 'Can this situation be dealt with later?' We can predict the anticipated consequences of the event and the necessity for continuity it may require.

This is a prospective outlook which is essential for anyone learning to prepare for change. Adopting this approach will prepare you to face up to all kinds of situations. It evaluates whether the present situation is likely to develop and if this indicates a threat or opportunity in the medium term.

Evolution is relative to:

– *the accuracy of information available* to evaluate the situation and its continuing circumstances.

– *the foreseeable shape* events will take, bearing in mind all the conditions surrounding the situation.

EXAMPLE

Is the instruction to reduce general expenditure a one-off demand with no other implications? Or does it imply the establishment of a new policy? If a new policy is being introduced then this is an area which needs careful observation from now on.

In your opinion, is this situation:

❏ *evolutionary?*

❏ *non-evolutionary?*

Once we are confronted with the problems that arise to undermine our organizational system, an objective view of the facts shows that the unpredictable may in reality quite often be predicted. We come to realize that we were either privy to information or in a position to obtain it. When we realize this, we can weigh up the importance of the present situation and avoid the risk of wasted effort.

RANKING PRIORITIES

These four factors contribute to giving perspective to the implications of an event in your professional environment. From there it is possible to clarify the most appropriate methods for handling the analyzed situation. Rapidly scanning the four areas with Yes/No type questions you will be in a position to order your priorities. If a situation responds to all four criteria, it obviously presents the maximum difficulty. You must act immediately in any given situation without recourse to existing deadlines and the risk of possible consequences on your results.

In handling the situation, you must also take into account two other factors: *ease of implementation and motivation to act.*

Most of us tend to favour activities that are easy to deal with. What is done can be struck off the list and it is very satisfying to watch the list getting shorter. The motivation to act naturally influences the process of ranking priorities. Pleasure generates efficiency. But beware: when we are enjoying a task we are apt to give too much time to it.

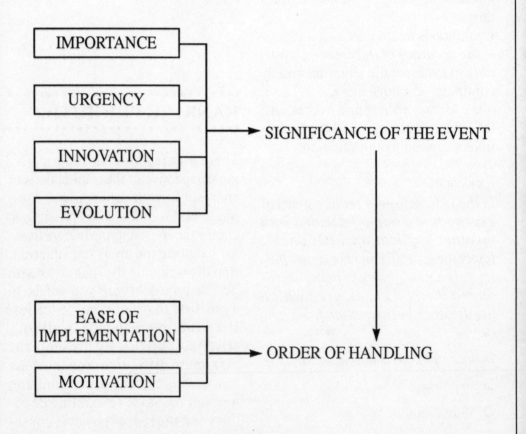

SIX ASPECTS OF A TASK

Importance

Does this situation need particular attention?

Are the stakes high in this situation and is there a direct relationship between this and your objectives and priorities?

If so, what is the result you wish to achieve and what is the deadline?

Urgency

Does this situation require immediate handling?

Looked at objectively, can the time limit be justified?

If so, is it up to me to act and in what time span?

Innovation

Does this situation fall under the category of routine handling?

Is there an internal formalized procedure responsible for it?

If so, does this method get results?

Evolution

Does this situation need delayed treatment?

Is there any element of information which could improve my capacity to anticipate developments?

If so, should we schedule an action or forecast a point of reference?

Ease of implementation

Does this activity require a minimum of time and energy?

Is this activity worth singling out for special consideration?

If so, is it wise to act now?

Motivation

Does this situation stimulate the interest and desire to act?

Could it influence my current or future results?

If so, when should I schedule its completion?

YOUR ORDER OF PRIORITIES

Situations	Important	Urgent	Innovative	Evolutionary	Easy	Motivating	Actions	Deadline
MD/Request for reduction of general expenditure				X	X		Checkpoints	Second half of the year
Customer/Request for information on product X			X				Plan product memo	Tuesday 24
SecurityServices/ Internal review		X					OK for Tuesday and Wednesday. Acknowledge receipt	
Commercial Managers/Meeting on product strategy	X			X		X	Prepare report	Monday 23

The questioning is specific and reinforces the objectivity of the judgement. In particular it demonstrates that urgent situations are far more rare than generally imagined and that some work procedures need adjustment. We should try to make this analysis an automatic reflex in our day-to-day working practice.

CONCLUSION

The handling of daily situations requires the use of tactics and action. It plays a determining role in how you manage your time . You need to aim at developing your ability to adapt if you wish to achieve this fundamental skill.

There is nothing more dangerous than action without thought. We can become bewildered by the amount going on and lose control of our activities. We may even become incapable of halting irreversible processes.

Taking time to think before acting is the key to personal organization. Treat yourself to some breathing space before going into action. If you do not make time for yourself how can you do so for others?

PRIORITIZE YOUR TIME

Section 7
FOLLOW-UP

> *'He who masters his time masters himself.'*
>
> VOLTAIRE

Management of priorities cannot be successful without an effective follow-up system. This system guarantees both constant monitoring (from day to day) and the distance necessary for evaluating events. It gives us an opportunity to highlight any strengths and pinpoint trends. Follow-up is as much a means of checking as anticipating. It is a link between current activity and what we need to ensure for the coming months.

In the sequence of action the follow-up system is often looked upon as a poor relation. Most of us prefer to invest our energy in exercising action and a bit less in its preparation. From experience, however, we find that continued success often depends on the efficiency of a follow-up system. How does a top ranking sports champion succeed if not by using the techniques of automatic control?

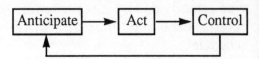

In the business world there is a lot to be gained from a reappraisal of automatic control. On an individual basis, our capacity for progress depends for the most part on ourselves.

THE THREE STAGES OF FOLLOW-UP

Consider your professional obligations and the difficulties which arise in controlling your own practices. Examine your systems and function as a whole under these three levels of scrutiny:

Level one: constant monitoring
This consists of analysing your activities from day to day, the gap between what was planned and what was actually done. This procedure requires the existence of a work schedule.

The conclusions obtained allow for immediate adjustments: carrying forward, delegating, cancelling, etc.

We can look for inspiration to a sport, in this case basketball, and discover that using frequent time-outs could be adopted by and beneficial to the business world. The aim is to break up the day with intermediate points, take into account the turn of events, and make provision for instructions to be relayed and/or precautions to be taken.

YOUR COMMENTS

Level two: respecting objectives
It is essential to keep a clear head and not become too preoccupied with small details. Our system of managing priorities will only succeed if we work towards consistency in the medium term. This brings us back to the action plan. The critical analysis it brings us shows whether or not we translate intentions into actions and whether the workload and rhythm are adapted to our level of availability. In certain instances it may be necessary to rethink the programme which has been chosen. The frequency of this follow-up should be monthly or fortnightly.

YOUR COMMENTS

Level three: evolution of key aspects
Going beyond operational objectives, it is sometimes useful to follow the development of key aspects of the functioning of your personal system of organization. For this purpose, we can use the concept of a Personal Dashboard. Just as with a car, you can use the dashboard to spot at a glance the level of activity (number of kms covered), the condition of the main components (oil pressure) or the performance obtained (speed).

CAN YOU CONTROL YOUR ACTIVITIES?

STATEMENTS	YES	NO
1. Study your practices. Does our concept of control rely on voluntary action rather than compulsion? Does the initiative depend on you rather than on your professional environment?		
2. You do not make use of a dashboard centred on your individual activities and performance.		
3. You don't take stock of your daily activities each morning or evening.		
4. You recognize the 20 per cent of tasks which generate 80 per cent of foreseeable time loss.		
5. In the course of the day you pause for a few moments of reflection, and revise your plans if necessary.		
6. Your methods of control are adapted to a practical approach to what's at stake.		
7. You regularly implement actions to regulate any flaws detected.		
8. You inform those around you (superiors, colleagues) of your findings and results.		
9. You plan reflection time into your schedule.		
10. You feel that everyone can constantly learn and progress.		
TOTAL		

The Yes replies assist you in the evaluation of the efficiency of your follow-up system. This gives you the opportunity to capitalize on your methods and techniques in this area.

On your Personal Dashboard, the indicators which you included, should correspond to key performances, to aspects which are difficult to pinpoint exactly, or to developmental areas about which you need objective information.

Some indicators will be more or less permanent whereas others may disappear after a few months. Follow-ups should usually recur at regular monthly intervals.

YOUR COMMENTS

....

....

CHOOSING INDICATORS

1. The indicators should be clear about the goals to be achieved. They are few in number (between 7-10) so only the most valuable information will be retained.

2. They can be placed before your work (amount of typing to be done) in relation to the work done (typing carried out, training) or the aftermath (assignments respecting time limits, percentage of work carried out within the time limits, etc).

3. They refer to a norm (12 hours, 95 per cent) but they may also be appreciated in the absolute. Remember that an isolated case or result has no value. It is only in the analysis of a trend (month after month) that we can monitor change.

4. The methods of measuring must be in line economically with the level of precision sought. In many cases a detailed analysis is not necessary. We should, however, select work units which are easy to calculate (number, percentage, etc).

5. It is essential to be thorough when collecting data. It is obvious that the method cannot be changed from one period to the next without the risk of modifying the results obtained. So settle on one method and stick to it.

EXAMINE YOUR PERSONAL DASHBOARD

Your personal dashboard is multifunctional. It is a device for controlling and deciding. It can be used in a preventative capacity as an aid to estimating.
To demonstrate the practical use of a personal dashboard look at the following example of a secretary working in an administrative service section.

INDICATORS	JAN	FEB	MAR	APR	MAY	JUNE
Inter-departmental coordination	5 days					
Errors in monitoring phone calls	25					
Average number of words per minute						
Typing workload						
Typing output						
Percentage of assignments meeting deadline						
Accuracy of records	95%					
Percentage of time given to training	12 hrs					
Overtime						

DRAWING UP A PERSONAL DASHBOARD

1. List the vital aspects of success
Include the relevant factors, (areas, situations, activities, tasks) and results (quality, cost, time limit) in the planning of your activity. This

does not concern your operational objectives: those immediate results are monitored elsewhere.
An analysis of the situation (section 2) should help you in this exercise, especially making a checklist and listing the tasks in rank order. Think of as many as possible. It will be easier afterwards to select those indicators you wish to retain:

1
2
3
4
5
6
7
8
9
10

In this list, identify the key aspects of your job, in other words, the information that represents a high degree of value.

LIST OF QUESTIONS

1. What can you do to increase the quality of service given?
Is there better correlation with customer needs?
Better adapted information?

2. What are the time limits and waiting periods?
The rate of use and/or availability of material?
Delays in relation to planning?

3. What level of respect is there for procedures and methods?
What slot do these basic procedures fill?
What are the main irregularities and their causes?

4. What can you say about the flexibility of existing
   communication channels?
Are there any bottlenecks?
How much time is essential for the administration of
   documents and materials used?

5. Can the consumption of materials and energy be reduced?
What is the level of waste?
What is the rate of recycling?

6. What are the working conditions like?
How do physical conditions measure up to the norm (noise,
   temperature, etc)?
What is the rate of interruptions in productivity?

7. What are the estimates for the main expenses in your job?
What are the main areas of waste?
What is the discrepancy between budget forecast and actual
   results?

8. What are the main quantities produced?
Are you getting/giving value for money?
What are the main cost prices (per period)?

2. Choosing measuring indicators

Determine the measuring indicator which best explains your need for information on each of the elements selected. The drafting of the indicator depends on the work unit chosen and the method of quantifying.

Establishing this can be approached in many ways. Billing errors can be expressed in terms of absolute values (150 errors), as a percentage of total operations (1.2 per cent), in terms of working hours necessary for correcting them (50 hours).

Choose the approach best adapted to your need for information (visibility and meaning of the action) and the easiest to measure (feasibility).

As an exercise attempt to write down all the indicators possible for the first task on your list.

1- ....

2- ....

3- ....

If you can't manage to find several possible indicators, this suggests that the area is still too vague. So break it down into uniform sub-groupings and choose the one which corresponds to your needs.

Our concern for measuring in economic terms leads us to use a procedure which highlights exceptions (only counting what appears outside the norm) or to reason based on statistical deductions (a few operations chosen at random).

3. Draw up your personal dashboard

Highlighting information implies the use of graphic representation. Nothing else is as effective in visualizing the evolution of a task or working procedure. But the essential quality of a Personal Dashboard rests on it being the synthesis of all the key elements of your working organizational system.

CREATE YOUR PERSONAL DASHBOARD

INDICATORS	JAN	FEB	MAR	APR	MAY	JUNE
1						
2						
3						
4						
5						
6						
7						
8						
9						
10						

Section 8
CONCLUSION

> *'The real riches are the methods.'*
> NIETZSCHE

Now that you've reached the end of this guide, it is time to put these methods to the test. It is never easy to challenge your own practices, but re-examining your working methods may lead to a solution to your working difficulties. Those expecting any magic or miracle cures will, of course, be disappointed but improvements should result in the short to medium term.

Managing priorities is not an exact science but a constant and dynamic process. It is a total system of organization around crucial points: current assignment and prioritizing of tasks; operational objectives and action plan; organization systems and evaluation of daily events; and, most importantly, follow-up.

This method constitues its own evolution. Every six to twelve months, it is necessary to examine the changes taking place in our environment and review our choice of priorities and operational objectives accordingly. This is at the heart of the reactor. There can be no tactical intelligence without first establishing a clear and realistic strategy. This gives meaning to your daily actions and offers the flexibility to cope with the necessary adaptations and modifications in the field. Your success depends now on using the proposed methods wisely. Are you prepared to go into action? Can you wave goodbye to those conscious and subconscious habits? All learning requires self-discipline and patience, together with a good dose of optimism.

WILL TO SUCCEED, KNOWLEDGE, ABILITY... This guide may provide the techniques but it is incapable of producing the determination to act.

The first condition of success requires you to identify your motives for this project: Why is it useful to manage priorities? What can you gain from it? The answers to these two questions are all-important for the progression of the operation.

Experience has given us a few good tips on the subject of implementation:

1. Act quickly

Don't wait too long to test these methods. The sooner the better. It is only by attempting to implement them that you can actually succeed! Experience is irreplaceable, and immediate action makes things seem much simpler than we imagined beforehand. Specify a period of experimentation right now, and set a date for your first review. Act now. There will be plenty of time for criticism and review afterwards.

2. Putting the test into perspective

Decide how sophisticated a method to use on the basis of your needs and personality. To elaborate on this guideline, try adopting this philosophy: he who dares, wins. It is up to you to decide the means to be used: the best being those you build yourself... Avoid the all or nothing approach . Everyone must decide their own rhythm. Step by step you can see the progress to be achieved. It is not unthinkable to begin with a daily work plan, then construct a personal dashboard. Nibbling in this way will give you an appetite for greater action. Each stage will give you the desire to push a little further.

3. Involve your colleagues

You cannot manage your priorities on the backs of others.

Your success depends on the cooperation of your colleagues. Make sure they understand what you're doing and feel it is worth their while getting involved.

Leading by example is a guarantee of success. Act efficiently and let it be noticed. Make it clear that the efficiency of one person is for the collective good and that the inverse is also true.

FURTHER READING FROM KOGAN PAGE

Be An Achiever, Geoffrey Moss, 1991

Don't Do. Delegate!, J M Jenks and J M Kelly, 1986

How to Get More Done, John and Fiona Humphrey, 1990

Individual Excellence, Phil Lowe and Ralph Lewis, 1992

Make Every Minute Count, Marion E Haynes, 1988

Managing Your Time, Lothar J Seiwert, 1989

Self-Empowerment, Sam R Lloyd and Christine Berthelot, 1992

Time is Money: Save It, Lothar J Seiwert, 1991

NOTES

PRIORITIZE YOUR TIME